TAKE OFF!

How Airplanes Work for Kids

BABY PROFESSOR

EDUCATION KIDS

LEARN ABOUT AIRPLANE!

People have always loved watching birds. We are trying to figure out how they fly. Birds make flying look easy.

Birds have hollow bones and feathers. Some people have always wanted to fly like birds. Humans tried to fly but they did not know how to.

Humans have
heavy bones
and no feathers.
We are not
designed to fly!
But people kept
finding a way
to soar high in
the sky.

It started with simple kites. After several years of trying, the Chinese were able to fly kites in the air. The Chinese invented the kite.

The Chinese invented kites for weather experiments. Kites are used for religious services too. Later it helped scientists understand about wind currents.

There were many other experiments with flying. It wasn't until the 20th century that people saw the first airplane. Orville and Wilbur Wright created the first successful flying machine. with the first flight on December 17, 1903.

And we have
moved on
from that day.
People invented
gliders, airships,
helicopters,
commercial .
And planes that
fly faster than
the speed of
sound.

Inventors continue designing new kinds of planes. They make mistakes and learn and keep pushing forward to make even better aircraft.

An airplane is
a fixed-wing
flying machine.
It is propelled
through the
air by engines.
Airplanes
are used for
transportation,
recreation,
research
and military
purposes.

Airplanes can
be so small
they only hold
one person.
It can be big
that hundreds
of people can
fly in them too.

The key to
keeping an
airplane flying
is the wings.
The plane flies
because the wing
is positioned at an
angle that pushes
downward on the
air. The propellers
move the plane
forward, the wing
splits the air and
pushes down on
the air that goes
below it.

There are four
forces that
affect things
that fly. They
are weight, lift,
drag, and thrust.
These four forces
are responsible
for making the
plane go up,
travel in the air,
and come down
again.

Thrust is the process that makes the airplane move forward. Engines provide the thrust needed to move a plane. Thrust propels a plane in the direction of motion.

Airplanes fly, instead of driving like cars. Airplanes are able to produce a force called lift. Lift moves the airplane upward.

Planes have
wings that
have a shape
called an airfoil.
It is important
because it
helps the plane
overcome
gravity. Because
of the airfoil
shape, air flows
faster over the
top than the
bottom.

As a result,
it creates a
higher pressure
underneath
the wing which
then pushes
the plane up.
The disturbed
air slows down
the plane as it
moves forward,
thus ensuring
balance.

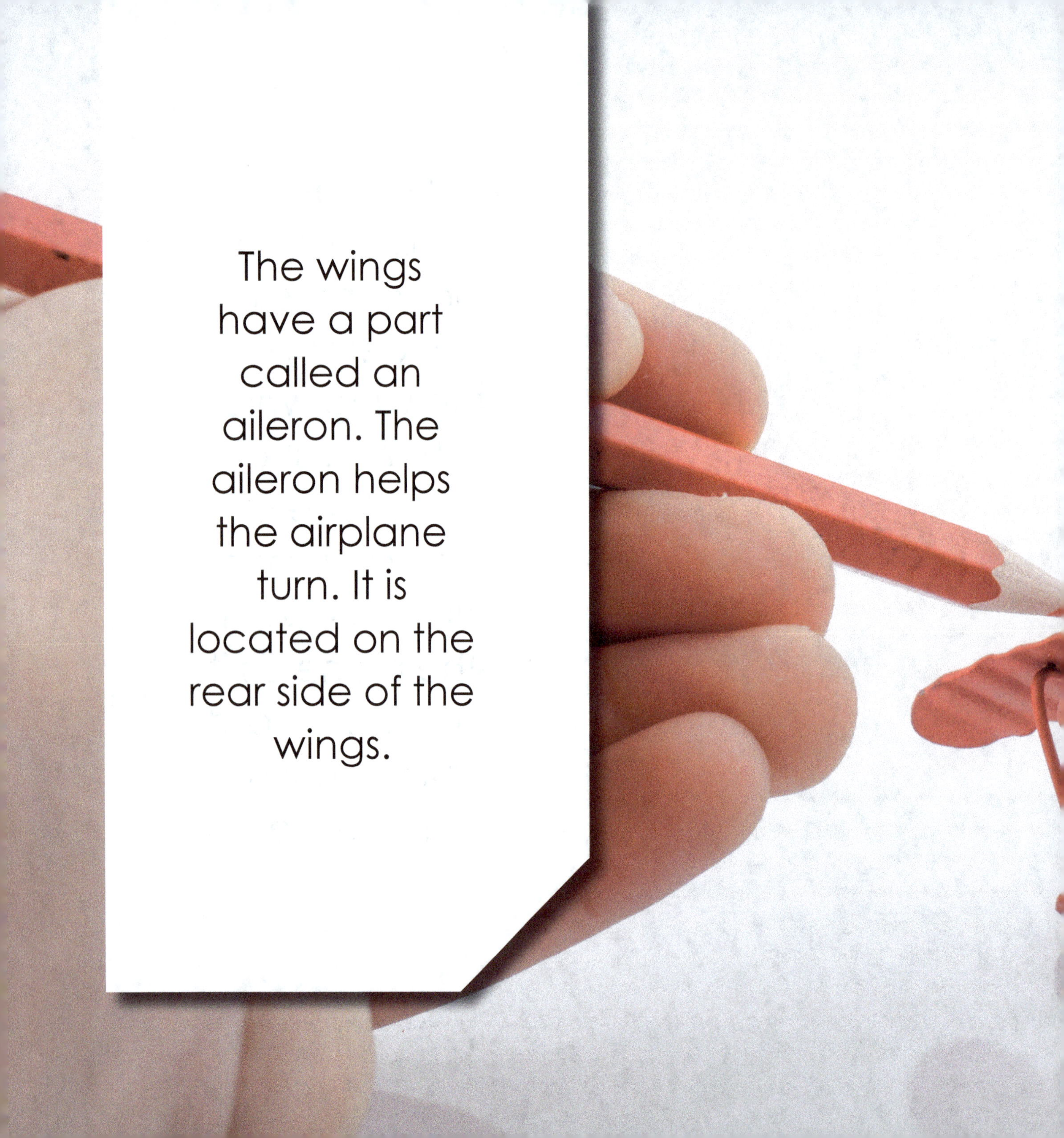

The wings
have a part
called an
aileron. The
aileron helps
the airplane
turn. It is
located on the
rear side of the
wings.

Planes defy gravity. Gravity is the invisible force that pulls everything down toward the Earth. When planes are flying it is defying this constant force.

Weight is the power of gravity. Gravity works in a downward direction; it pulls you towards the center of the earth. If you jump up from the floor, gravity works on the mass of your body to draw you back down again.

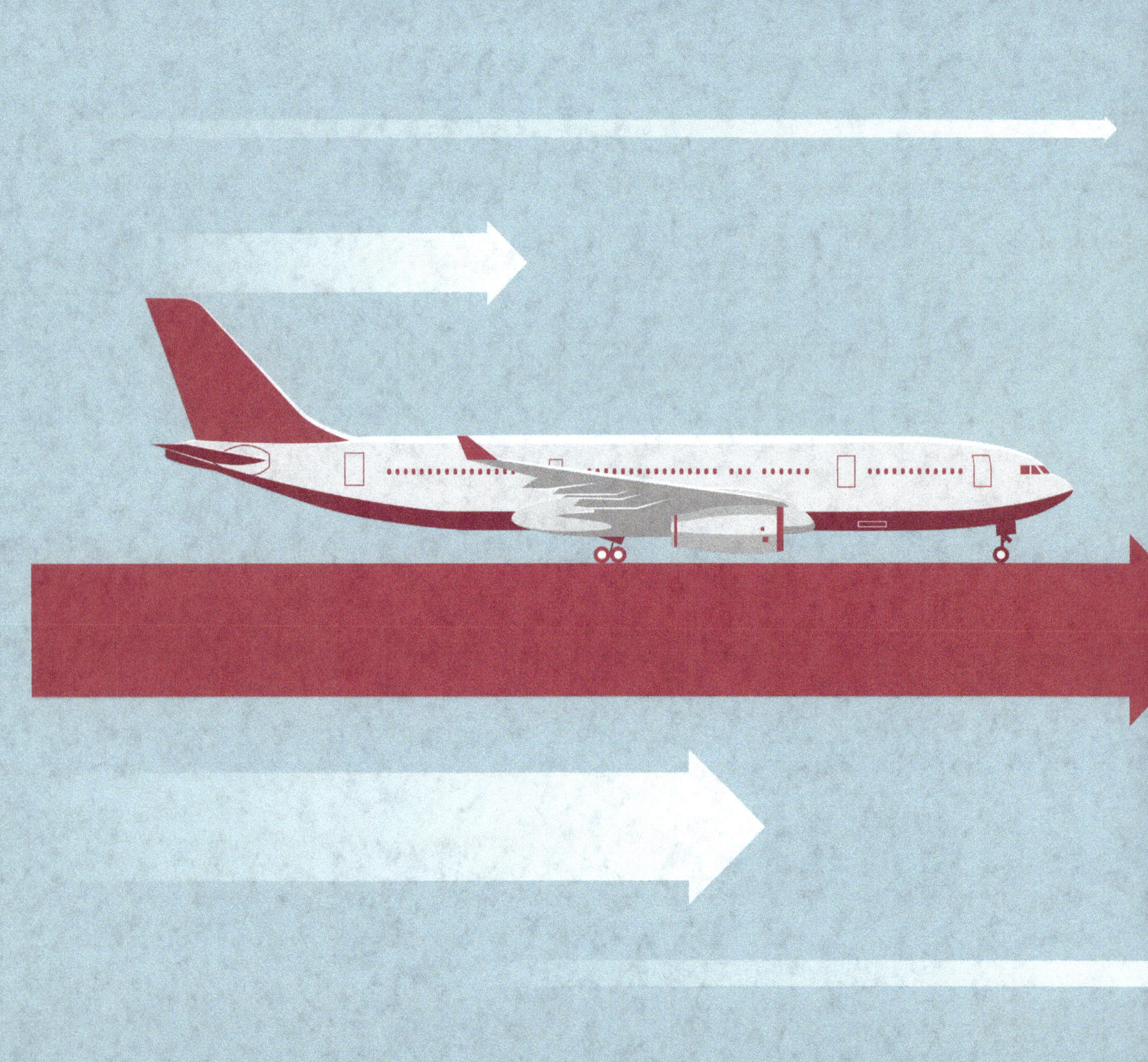

There is a force
that slows down
the forward
movement
of the plane,
called Drag.
Drag is caused
by friction
between the
moving object
and the air
around it.
Drag can also
be called air
resistance.

The long, thin body of an aircraft is called the fuselage. It is the central part of an airplane that carries the crew, passengers and cargo. It is often called the main part of the airplane.

EXIT
EXIT

Where does the pilot go? Pilots control the plane from the cockpit. The cockpit is located at the front of the fuselage. The cockpit of a plane is full of flight instruments with different controls and monitors to watch.

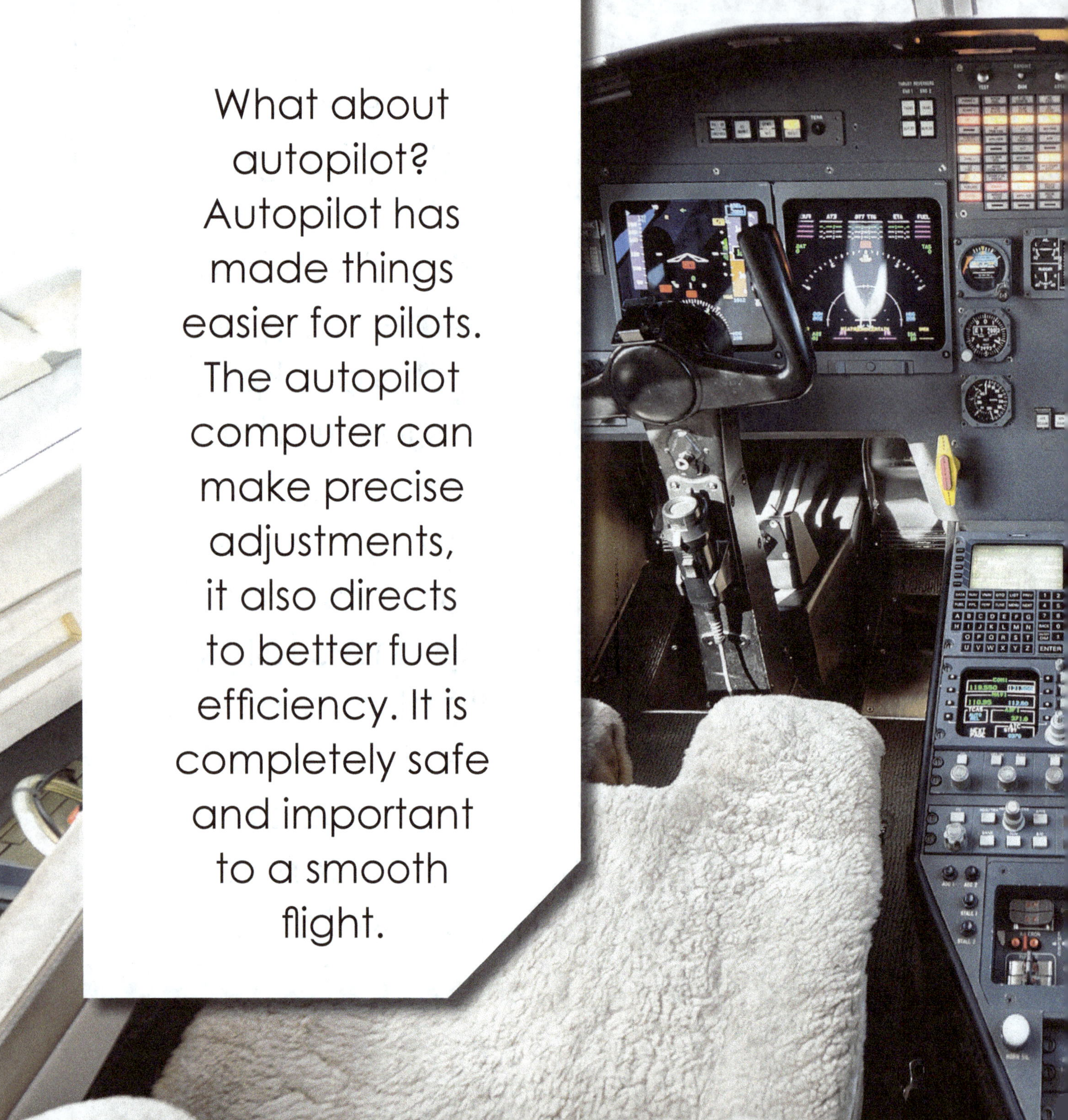

What about autopilot? Autopilot has made things easier for pilots. The autopilot computer can make precise adjustments, it also directs to better fuel efficiency. It is completely safe and important to a smooth flight.

RADIO CALL T7-NIK
SELCAL JO-KM
LEAD ACID
BATTERY
INSTALLED
BATTERY TEMP.
SYSTEM
DISABLED

There are two main types of airplanes: propeller driven planes and jet planes. Both are still flying machines that transport us from places but with thrust generated in different ways.

Propeller driven planes uses propellers turned by an engine. It is a device with two or more blades that turn quickly to push the air back over the wings and help the aircraft move.

Jet planes
do not have
propellers.
Instead they
use jet engines
to move
the airplane
forward. A jet
plane flies much
faster and can
climb higher in
the sky than the
propeller planes.

The only living
things capable
of powered
flight are insects,
birds and bats.
True flight is
achieved by
these animals.
Because they
are using their
wings.

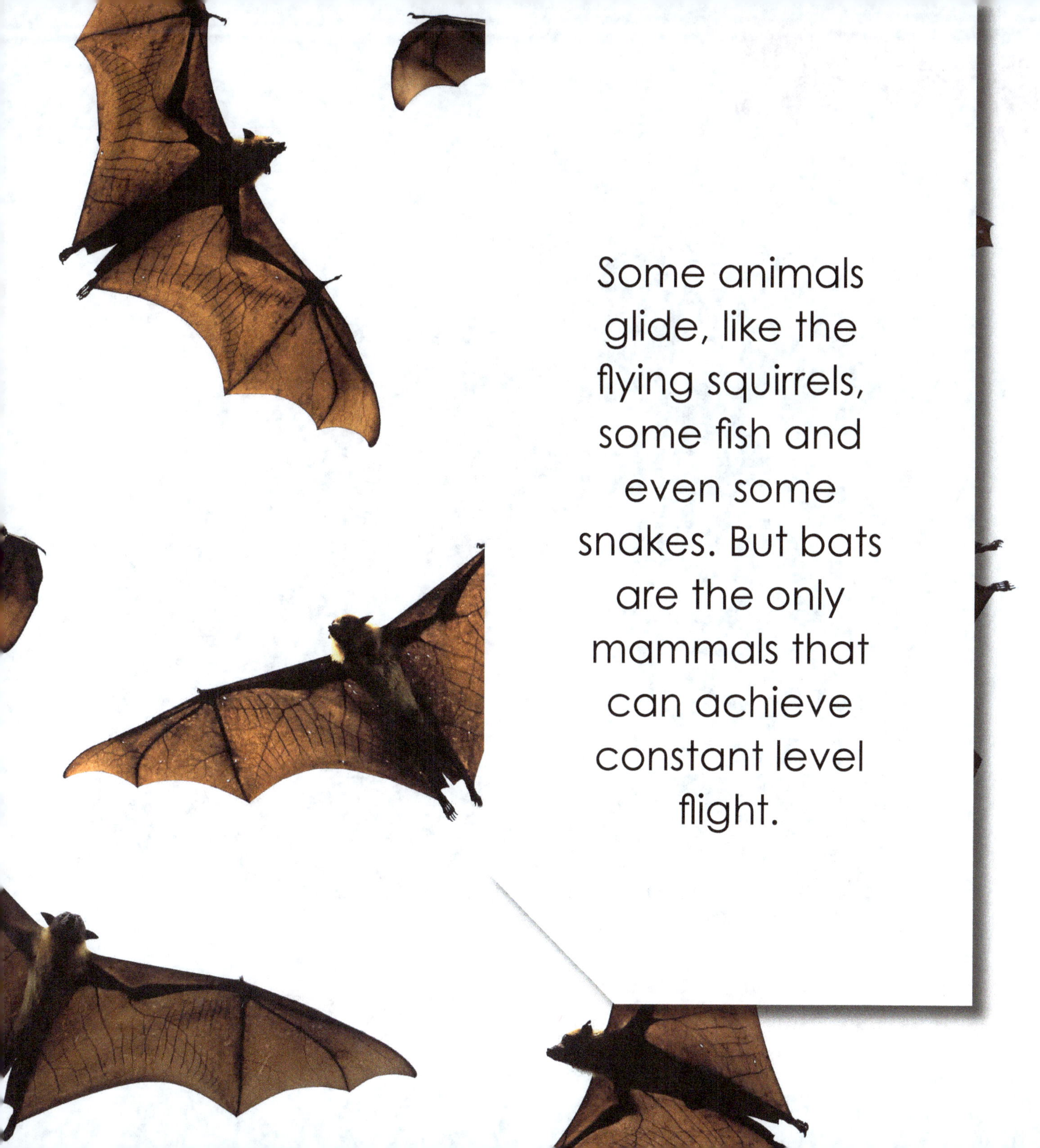

Some animals glide, like the flying squirrels, some fish and even some snakes. But bats are the only mammals that can achieve constant level flight.

Visit
BABY PROFESSOR
EDUCATION KIDS
www.BabyProfessorBooks.com
to download Free Baby Professor eBooks and view
our catalog of new and exciting Children's Books